LEVEL 2 SCIENCE
LET'S READ AND FIND OUT

RUNNING ON SUNSHINE

HOW DOES SOLAR ENERGY WORK?

BY CAROLYN CINAMI DeCRISTOFANO

ILLUSTRATED BY GIOVANA MEDEIROS

HARPER

An Imprint of HarperCollinsPublishers

Special thanks to Dr. Bart Bartlett, Associate Professor of Chemistry at the University of Michigan, for his valuable assistance.

The Let's-Read-and-Find-Out Science book series was originated by Dr. Franklyn M. Branley, Astronomer Emeritus and former Chairman of the American Museum of Natural History–Hayden Planetarium, and was formerly co-edited by him and Dr. Roma Gans, Professor Emeritus of Childhood Education, Teachers College, Columbia University. Text and illustrations for each of the books in the series are checked for accuracy by an expert in the relevant field. For more information about Let's-Read-and-Find-Out Science books, write to HarperCollins Children's Books, 195 Broadway, New York, NY 10007, or visit our website at www.letsreadandfindout.com.

Let's Read-and-Find-Out Science® is a trademark of HarperCollins Publishers.

Library of Congress Control Number: 2017951097
ISBN 978-0-06-247311-0 (trade bdg.) — ISBN 978-0-06-247310-3 (pbk.)

The artist used Adobe Photoshop to create the digital illustrations for this book.
Typography by Erica De Chavez 18 19 20 21 22   SCP   10 9 8 7 6 5 4 3 2 1 ❖ First Edition

With love to my always supportive husband, Barry, and to dear friends, readers, and cheerleaders Corri and Rebecca Taylor. You all keep me running on your sunshine—C.C.D.

The author would like to thank the following colleagues who provided early feedback and support for this book: Katy Laguzza; Jaime Martinez; REcharge Labs' Mike Arquin and Asia Ward; Campus School of Carlow University educators Susan Ament, Stephanie Conrad, Jennifer Filak, and Julie Marcoux; and Chris Boyer, Executive Director of the National Association for Search and Rescue.

For my family—G.M.

Far from Earth, a giant, fiery ball flings flame-like fingers into space. Its superhot surface glows, sloshes, and swirls. The Sun simply *cannot* contain all its **energy**. Some energy escapes as a constant flow of heat and light. That's sunshine!

See this one little stream of sunshine? Follow it as it zooms toward Earth, whizzing through space so fast it covers 93 million miles in 8 minutes, 18 seconds flat.

Follow it down,

down,

down!

Ping!

Maybe the sunlight strikes one single spot on one green leaf. When that happens—

Zing!

Tiny parts inside the leaf, much too small to see, kick into action. A superb sun catcher, the leaf bundles the Sun's energy into little packages, storing it for later. The plant will need this energy to grow and stay alive.

BITE INTO A MELON.

Mmmm . . . sweet! That's the taste of bundled sunshine. It's sugar, a combination of energy from the Sun and materials from air and water.

Or maybe the sunshine strikes something else instead. Like a leaf, this something catches the Sun's energy. But it's not a leaf. Shiny, smooth, hard, and flat, it is made from a special glass. This sun catcher is a **solar panel**. Solar panels catch solar energy.

Maybe you have seen solar panels before. They're popping up in fields, on rooftops, and in lots of other places. What is the solar energy used for?

Lots of things!

For example, the captured sunshine helps things go.

Look! Up in the sky, it's not a bird . . . and it's no ordinary plane. . . .

It's a super solar plane! With the help of solar panels, sunlight powers its flight around the world.

This plane, *Solar Impulse 2*, made the first round-the-world flight powered by solar energy in 2016.

Sunshine and solar panels keep these cars on the go. They drive nearly 2,000 miles in a cross-country race between Australia's north and south coasts, all without a single drop of gasoline.

75

22

16

4

STA

Solar energy and solar panels can also power the freezer in an ice-cream truck! How cool is that?

14

Clipped to rescue workers' backpacks, bendy solar panels do more serious work. They use sunshine to charge the rescuers' phones. Even far from towns and cities, they stay connected.

Day by sunny day, more and more gadgets and machines are running on sunshine. This is a big deal! It helps avoid problems with how we usually power machines. But . . . what *is* the usual way?

Say you want some toast. Your toaster needs **electricity**. Where does it come from?

Maybe from the wall, where the toaster is plugged in?

Nope. Plugs connect to wires that are behind the walls, but wires are like roads that electricity travels on. These wires are the end of a long path from electricity's starting point.

Well, not *exactly*—but fires send out smoke and other stuff. This can make the air unhealthy to breathe. It also leads to changes in weather patterns all around the world. Surprising rains drench some places, but rain does not fall where it's expected. Cold snaps freeze and heat waves sizzle like never before. Yikes! We want electricity, but we don't want what comes with those fires!

SEVERE RAINFALL
EXTREME WEATHER

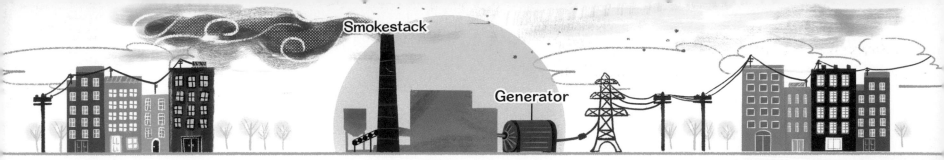

Smokestack

Generator

Here, inside a power station, mighty machines called **generators** make electricity flow. Here's how the system usually works:

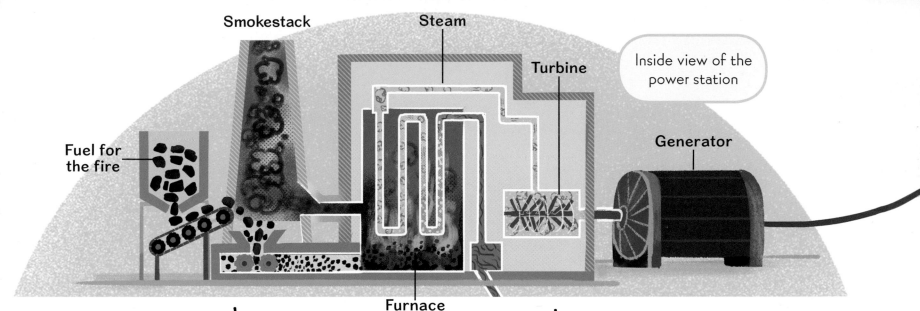

Smokestack

Steam

Turbine

Inside view of the power station

Fuel for the fire

Generator

Furnace

Sssssssssssss!

Fires heat containers of water in a furnace—like giant teakettles. The hissing steam escapes and flows through pipes.

Bump!

The steam hits a moving part called a turbine. This makes the turbine spin. The spinning part makes magnets and wires in the generator move. Electricity flows. But there's trouble.

These fires have bad breath!

What could we use?

Hmm . . . We need to use energy without making the air dirty.

Let's see. . . . (You know already, don't you?)

Sunshine!

Yes! But we can't just plug into the Sun. That's where solar panels come in.

Remember the leaf, the Sun, the *ping* and the *zing*? Something similar happens inside a solar panel.

Ping!
Sunlight strikes.
Zing!
Teeny-tiny parts inside the glass, much, *much* too small to see, kick into action. Such teeny-tiny bits, called **electrons**, are in everything you touch, but the glass is specially made so its electrons respond in an important way.

When sunlight strikes this glass, its electrons flutter. Their hubbub stirs *other* electrons—the ones in wires connected to the panel. They jiggle and jostle, like kids fidgeting in a line, passing the Sun's energy from one electron to another. It's one long shiver of energy. It's electricity!

This electricity flows all the way to people's homes, maybe even yours. *Pop!* *This* toast is made with sunshine!

Back at the solar panel, the Sun keeps shining. *Ping, zing*, flutter, shiver. Electricity keeps flowing. This electricity powers our machines as usual, only without fires and the troubles they can bring.

This is good news, but there are some tricky things about using solar energy.

What happens when it rains?
Or when clouds block the Sun?
Or when snow covers the solar panel?
Or at night?!

Without sunlight, solar panels can't do their job!
Uh-oh.
Now what?

Engineers are people who solve problems. It's their job to figure out "now what."

Some of them are working on ways to store solar energy for later. For example, we might use rechargeable batteries, like the ones in cell phones. It would take a whole lot of space to hold the batteries for a whole town's electricity. Some engineers work on smaller batteries, but other engineers are trying different ideas.

Solar panels

Dam

Pool of water

Nighttime

Daytime

Pump

Underground generators

Whirrrrr. Whirrrr.

Pumps that run on sunshine help store solar energy for nighttime.

Here's how.

By day, solar panels generate electricity. Electricity runs the pumps.

The pumps lift tons of water up to a giant pool with a dam.

At night . . . *Whoosh!* A dam opens. A high-energy rush of water flows down until—

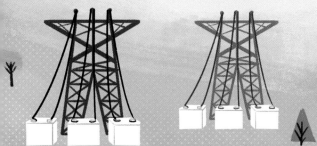

Bump! The water hits a turbine. This makes the generator's magnets and wires move. Electricity flows even at night, but without steam and without fires. Day, up. Night, down. Water rises, storing energy. Water falls, releasing energy.

Storing solar energy isn't enough. Collecting as much as possible is also important—but how?

Sun-tracking solar panels are one idea. Like sunflowers, they turn and always face the Sun, catching energy all day.

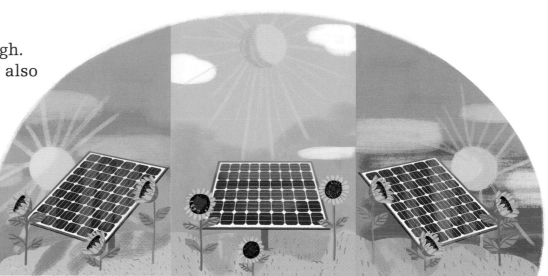

Think how much sunlight falls on rooftops every day. Imagine the possibilities if these were solar collectors! Sometimes they are.

Instead of being placed on a roof, these solar panels *are* the roof. With solar panel shingles, the roof does double duty, providing protection and power.

A lot of sunshine also falls on roads. Engineers are experimenting with paving roads with super-strong solar panels. Some solar roads have built-in extras. For example, lights turn on when animals are in the road. This helps keep everyone safe.

Gas engines burn gasoline, but solar-powered electric engines run on sunshine.

With sunlight, solar panels make electricity flow, but there are other ways to use sunshine.

For example, we can use sunshine to heat things up.

In some sunny places around the world, some people are using new solar cookers instead of cooking food with fires.

Solar walls are a kind of twist on this idea. The walls soak up sunshine. At night, when they release energy into the building, they make the indoors warm and cozy.

Around the world, people have put solar energy to work. But some ideas are not yet ready.

Remember the special solar-powered plane and race cars? Today, they are amazing experiments. Maybe when you are older, most cars and passenger planes will run on sunshine.

In the future, you might wear clothes woven from special plastic threads, which operate like solar panels. You won't just get into these clothes. You'll also plug into them.

You might look out windows that are actually see-through solar panels.

Someday, blind people might see with the help of tiny **solar chips** placed in their eyes.

Solar **technologies** are fun to think about. They're exciting, and they're important. Using solar energy won't solve everything, but it avoids some big problems. The energy from sunshine helps people, and it doesn't pollute.

We need even more creative ideas to make solar energy work better and better. So, what can *you* dream up? Grab a snack of bundled sunlight. Then let your imagination run—on sunshine.

FIND OUT MORE

REFLECT ON SOLAR ENERGY!

To collect energy from the Sun, it sometimes helps to focus sunlight, or direct it from a few different places to one small spot. Mirrors can help focus the light. See how focusing sunlight could help a solar cooker work.

YOU NEED:

- Small mirrors, such as the ones in makeup containers
- Pebble
- Blocks
- Play dough
- Optional: Aluminum foil and cardboard or mylar (shiny, silvery balloon material)
- A bright, sunny spot (can be a sidewalk or a shelf near a window)
- Two small, clear plastic cups, two similar ice cubes
- Clock or watch

Do not look directly at the sun. Make sure you have permission to use the mirrors.

AIMING THE LIGHT

Explore how mirrors reflect, or redirect, light.

. . . .

1. Hold a mirror in one hand so it faces the Sun. Change the mirror's position slightly. Watch for a bright spot of light bouncing off the mirror onto something nearby—perhaps the ground, a wall, or your pants.
2. Move the mirror slowly. Can you make the light shine on the pebble? Explore! Try different arrangements.

FOCUSING LIGHT

Now try focusing a lot of light in one place. You can use the focused light to melt an ice cube fast.

. . . .

1. Place two small plastic cups next to each other in your sunny location. Make sure the Sun shines into each cup.
2. Now arrange the mirrors around one cup so they reflect as much sunlight into this cup as possible. Use blocks to raise the mirrors and play dough to keep them in place. You might add other shiny materials, like the aluminum foil, to help bounce even more sunshine into the cup.
3. When you have focused the sunlight in this cup, place an ice cube in each cup. For the cup with the mirrors, make any final changes so the focused sunlight shines on the cube.
4. Time how long it takes for each ice cube to melt, or see whether one melts more in a certain amount of time. Why do you think it happens this way?

GLOSSARY

Electricity: Energy related to electrons' motion, often in a wire, used to power many machines and similar technologies

Electron: One of the tiniest bits of stuff (or matter) that exists

Energy: What it takes to do work or make changes happen. Light, electricity, sound, and motion are examples of energy.

Engineer: A person whose job it is to use science, math, and his or her ideas to solve problems—by inventing and improving objects and ways of getting things done. Engineers create and improve different technologies.

Generator: A machine that makes electricity flow

Pump: A machine made for pushing or pulling water (or materials like water)

through tubes or pipes, moving the water from one location to another

Solar: Having to do with the Sun

Solar chip: A tiny object, or technology, that works a lot like a solar panel

Solar panel: A flat object, usually made of a special glass, made to change the Sun's energy to electricity

Solar wall: A type of heater that is part of a building's outer wall, specially made to take in solar energy and release heat energy into the building

Technology: Anything people create to help solve problems, get jobs done, or make tasks easier.

Turbine: An object that spins and makes a generator's magnets and wires move.

Be sure to look for all of these books in the Let's-Read-and-Find-Out Science series:

This book aligns with the Next Generation Science Standards.
Find out more at nextgenscience.org.

This book meets the Common Core State Standards for Science
and Technical Subjects. For Common Core resources for this title
and others, please visit www.readcommoncore.com.